WWII

THE GREATEST GENERATION'S
BOOK OF BLUE HUMOR

UNABRIDGED & UNCENSORED

Edited by

Daniel D. O'Tool

www.postmortempublications.com

Library of Congress Control Number: 2009930575

ISBN 978-0-615-30090-0

"We are not retreating--we are advancing in another direction."

~General Douglas MacArthur

"No good decision was ever made in a swivel chair."

~General George S. Patton, Jr.

Contents

Introduction

These words are an authentic compendium of poems, stories, one-liners, and anecdotes circulated throughout the World War II period by the men and women in the armed services as well as those in the factories and support services of the greatest war machine ever built.

This raucous humor is especially poignant in its representation of a nation's young finding levity in their most basic needs, displacing themselves from the reality of death. Each joke, story, witticism, poem, or amusement has been associated with a bonafide United States war poster of the day, reflecting its comparative humor.

In honoring the Greatest Generation for their sacrifices, these works are a testament to their dignity: that when faced with their own mortality, they still could laugh.

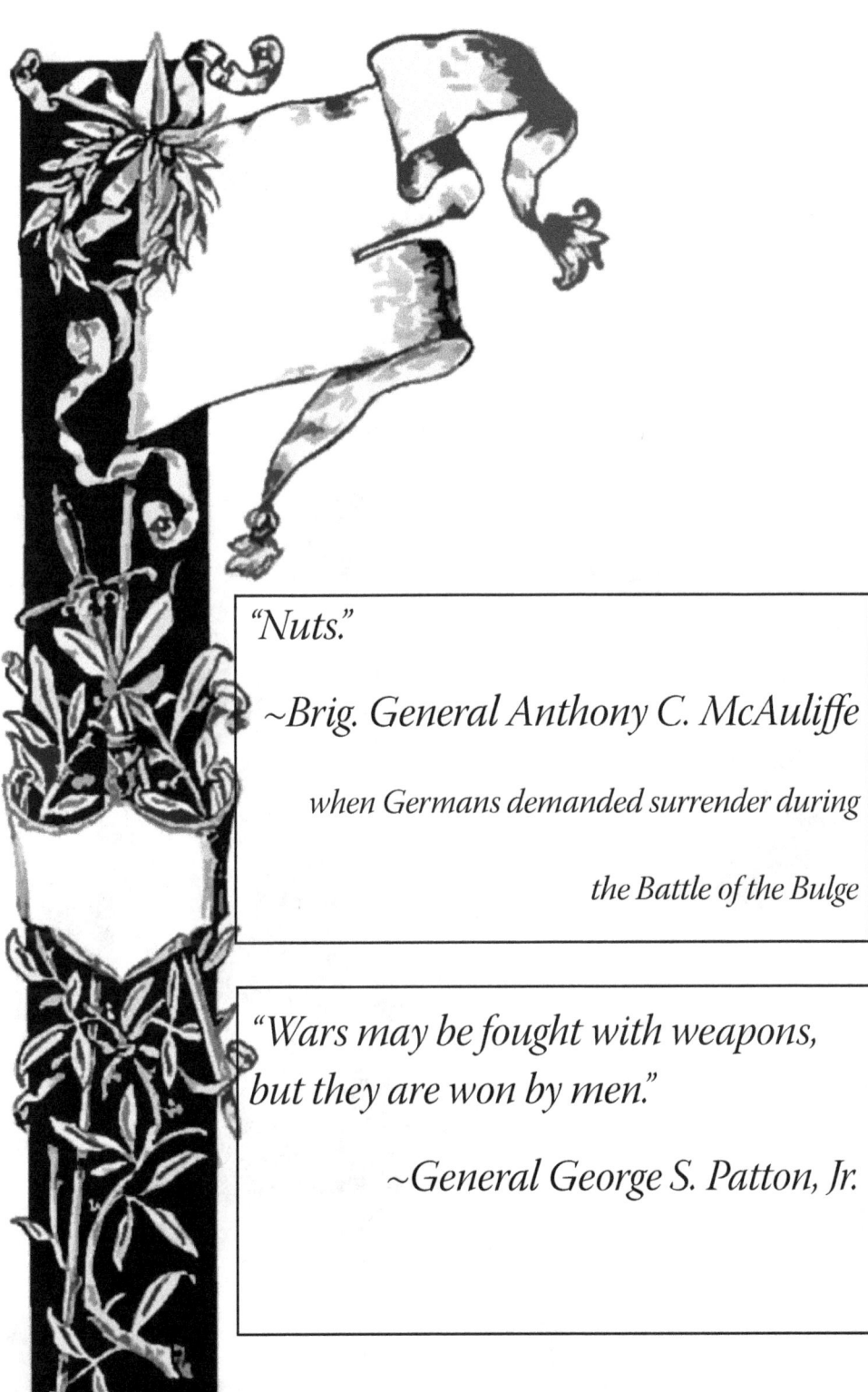

"Nuts."

~Brig. General Anthony C. McAuliffe

when Germans demanded surrender during

the Battle of the Bulge

"Wars may be fought with weapons,
but they are won by men."

~General George S. Patton, Jr.

4

It Happened One Night

Her name was Grace, she was one of the best,
So that night I put her through the test.
She looked so pretty, so sweet, so slim,
And the night was dark, the lights were dim.

I was so excited, my heart missed a beat,
For I knew I was in for a damn good treat.
I've seen her stripped, I've seen her bare,
I've felt her once, everywhere.

I got inside her, she screamed with joy,
That was the first night, boy oh boy.
I got up as quickly as I could,
I handled her gently, I knew she was good.

I rolled her over on her side,
Then on her back I also tried.
She was one big thrill, the best in the land,
The "P-38" of the fighter command.

WAVES, Description of

FROM: Executive Office, United States Naval Training School Dartmouth College, Hanover, N.H.

TO: WHOM IT MAY CONCERN.

Subject: WAVES, Description of:

1.   Commissioned 1943, approximately 200 in the class, average displacement 120, overall length 65 inches, beam 26 inches, launched at night.

2.   Twin mounts forward, single scupper below, dual purpose, has single torpedo tube, adjustable to fit torpedoes up to 8 inches, lightly armored, but deceptive, multiple screw propeller or propulsion, powered by reciprocating engines with unlimited output. Output varies directly with input. Fitted with gas injection tube aft for use at all times.

3.   Bluff in the counter, must be anchored with care, ammunition and cruising range unlimited, flies "baker" once a month, thermal efficiency very high, friction and findage loss negligible. Will stand very rough pitch and roll. Drive shaft well greased.

4.   May be driven for short time at forced draft; trim lines when full dressed, but more attractive when stripped for action. It is easy to contact, generally carries an officer aboard. Commanding officer subject to change without any notice. Should be scraped when barnacles appear. Seldom needs overhaul as it has self lubricating bearings.

5.   Torpedo tube must be primed for firing, and must be opened with care as it is hard to handle without expert manipulation. Hold may be expanded to several times normal size. Most effective when operating alone, and not with force or fleet. May be carrying small boat in hold after heavy engagement.

I.M. Hornie
By Direction

One Copy to All Officers.

ENLIST IN THE
WAVES

RELEASE A MAN TO FIGHT AT SEA

Apply to your nearest
NAVY RECRUITING STATION OR OFFICE OF NAVAL OFFICER PROCUREMENT

The Ditty Bag

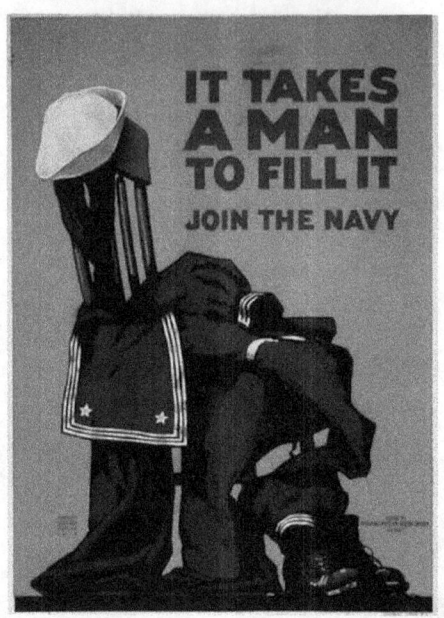

I'd like to ride the waves,
I'd like to ride the billows,
I'd rather ride a blushing bride
With her ass propped up on pillows.

☆

Last night as I lay on my bed
I dreamed my love and I were wed,
She turned to me and softly said,
 "Do it."

As she blushed, my rapture rose,
I lifted up her underclothes,
She whispered, "Darling, no one knows,
 "Do it."

It was a dream so short and sweet,
As I awoke in sweated heat,
And found that there upon the sheet,
 "I dood it."

There was a young man named Scott,
Who took a young girl on his yacht,
He was too tired to rape her
So he made darts of paper,
And languidly cast at her twat.

☆

Said the choir girl under the pew
To the sexton as he withdrew,
 "The vicar is quicker
And thicker and slicker
And three inches longer than you."

☆

Mary had a little skirt,
She stood against the light,
Who gives a damn for Mary's lamb
With Mary's claves in sight?

The Jones Brothers

Joe and John were twins, alike in every way, and only their very close friends could tell one from the other.

Now John was married and Joe was single. Joe was the proud owner of an old dilapidated rowboat, and, strangely enough, the day that John's wife died, Joe's boat sank.

A few days later, a kind old lady met Joe on the street and, mistaking him for John, said, "I'm sorry to hear of your misfortune. You must feel terrible." Just then Joe broke in and said, "I'm not a bit sorry; she was a rotten old thing from the start. Her bottom was all chewed out and smelled like old dead fish."

"The first time I got into her she made water faster than anything I ever saw. She had a crack in her back and a pretty bad hole in front, and every time I used her the hole kept getting bigger and bigger. But I got so I could handle her all right, but when anyone else used her she leaked like hell."

"But this is what really finished her. Four men from the other side of town came down and asked if I would rent her. I did. But I warned them what she was like and they said they didn't care. Being overanxious and surprised at me for renting her, they all tried getting in her at once and it was too much. She cracked in the middle and her bottom fell out."

Just then the old lady fainted.

9

Letters of Engagement

A soldier having returned to camp after furlough, received this letter from his girlfriend.

M is for the many times you made me.
O is for the other times you tried.
T is for those tourist cabin weekends.
H is for the hell that's in your eyes.
E is for the everlasting lovelight.
R is for the wreck you made of me.

Put them all together, they spell mother, and that's what I expect to be.

The soldier's reply to his girlfriend was:

F is for your funny little letter.
A is for my answer to your note.
T is for your tearful accusation.
H is for your hope that I'm the goat.
E is for the ease with which I made you.
R is for the wreck you thought I'd be.

Put them all together, they spell father, and you're crazy if you think it's me!

"I've found the job where I fit best!"

FIND YOUR WAR JOB
In Industry – Agriculture – Business

The Troubles of a Toolshop Girl

My job is full of troubles, and I'll relate a few,
Of some unpleasant little things which I am forced to do.
And if I wasn't naturally a virtuous young miss,
I wouldn't even hold my job long enough to tell you this.

A dozen times in any day, my modesty is shocked,
And I'm thankful that the tool crib door is most securely locked;
For the fellows crowd around like a lot of crazy fools,
While I'm busy every minute with the handling of their tools.

I don't mind the decent tools such as wrenches, drills, and shears,
But the tools these fellows ask me for make me blush behind the ears;
Like a guy repairing bearings might ask to see my balls,
And I don't recover from the shock before another calls.

They ask for cocks to put on pipes, for counterbores and bits,
But when they ask me for a screw, it almost scares me into fits;
For reamers to enlarge their holes, at least that's what they say,
They ask me if I've any nuts, more than a hundred times a day.

They ask me for a ratchet drill or for a bastard file,
And dirty things like "Bitch Dogs" which make my temper wild.
They ask me for a female gauge, and it almost makes me wail,
When they know I've never learned to tell a female from a male.

One fellow finds his tool too short, and another his too long,
A third one finds his tool too weak, and another his too strong.
One fellow asked me if I can put him wise to any good tail stock,
While another wanted a bunch of waste to wipe a plumber's cock.

The foreman looking around one day for a tool to cut and slot,
Asked me to open up my drawers and show him what I've got.
A dirty old machinist, lugging with half a "jag"
Demanded that I give to him a handful of my rag.

And once a fellow came to me, as I returned from lunch,
And asked me through the window, if I saw his big "Prick Punch."
Things like that annoy me, but I never shall forget
How that wretched millwright asked me if I had my monthly yet.

I didn't know till later that he meant the monthly blade,
So I gave him such a calling down, that I quickly made him fade.
All this merely goes to prove, as you surely must have known,
That a poor hardworking tool crib girl has troubles of her own.

A Twelve-Pound Gold Nugget

In a nursing district a Mrs. Brown presented her husband with a twelve-pound boy. Mr. Brown was so delighted that he told newspaper offices that he found a twelve-pound nugget of gold as good as any in America. Naturally the newspaper sent a reporter to get the particulars as every one was prospecting for gold in the little town where this happened. The reporter knocked on the door and pretty Mrs. Brown came to the door and the following interview took place:

He: Does Mr. Brown live here?
She: He does.
He: I understand he found a twelve-pound nugget of gold.
She: (seeing the joke) Yes, that's right.
He: Can you show me the exact spot where it was found?
She: I'm afraid that Mr. Brown would object as that is private.
He: Is the hold very far from here?
She: No, --'er quite near. -
He: Has Mr. Brown been working the claim long?
She: Just about nine months.
He: Was Mr. Brown the first one to work the claim?
She: He thinks so.
He: Has he reached the bottom yet?
She: Not yet but very nearly.
He: Do you think there are any more nuggets?
She: Yes, there ought to be if properly worked.
He: Has he worked the claim since he found the nugget?
She: No, but I told him last night it was time to start again.
He: I suppose he works it secretly?
She: Oh yes, mostly at night.
He: Do you help him any?
She: I do my level best.
He: Do you think he would sell the claim?
She: I doubt very much whether he would.
He: Does anyone else help him?
She: Certainly not, he gets to much pleasure working it himself.
He: Did he blast with glycerine?
She: No, he greased his tool with vaseline and dug in.
He: Has he widened the hole any?
She: Yes a little.
He: How large is the hole?
She: About normal size I suppose.

He: Is he going to improve the mine any?

She: Yes, he said he was going to whitewash the shaft tonight.

He: Does he work the claim alone at night?

She: No, I hold the tool for him and we go fifty-fifty.

He: Is he an expert in that line?

She: Well, he does very good work.

He: Would you mind showing me the nugget?

She: Certainly not. Then she brought in the twelve-pound baby boy.

The reporter collapsed and had to be taken to a hospital!!!!!

WEARING DIFFERENT UNIFORMS BUT WE ALL HAVE THE SAME BIG JOB — LET'S KEEP 'EM PULLING FOR VICTORY

Does Advertising Pay?

A woman about seven months pregnant got on the streetcar and sat down. She noticed a man opposite her smiling; being humiliated she moved to another seat. This time his smile turned into a grin. She changed her seat again, and he seemed even more amused. On the fourth change he burst out laughing, so she complained to the conductor and had the man arrested.

The case came up in court, and the judge asked the man if he had anything to say. "Well," he replied, "it was like this your honor. When the lady came in I couldn't help noticing her condition. She sat under a sign which read: "Gold dust twins are coming," and I had to smile to myself. Then she sat under a sign reading: "Use Sloans liniment to reduce the swelling." When she placed herself beneath the sign "Williams stick did this," I couldn't hold myself in. The fourth time she moved she sat below: "United States rubber would have prevented this accident" and I laughed out loud."

After hearing the man's argument, the judge declared, "Case dismissed!"

The Race at BVD Downs

Syracuse, N.Y.
Aviation Division
Series 43

Date: April 1, 1943

Ninth Race

Midnight Special

Entries:

Passionate Lady	4 To 1
Silk Panties..	4 to 1
Bare Belly	4 To 1
Conscience	20 To 1
Heavy Bosom	6 To 1
Merry Widow...	30 To 1
Jockey Shorts..	50 To 1
Clean Sheets..	3 To 1
Thighs	3 To 1
Big Dick(Favorite)	3 To 1

Purse: $10,000
Eligible: 18 years or over
Weather: Cloudy
Track Conditions: Soft & Spongy

They're off! Conscience is left at the post. Silk Panties and Jockey Shorts are off with a rush. Bare Belly shows. Heavy Bosom is being pressed hard. Passionate Lady and Thighs are now working hard. Merry Widow is caught between Thighs and Big Dick, and Clean Sheets is in a dangerous condition.

At the half, it's Bare Belly on top. Thighs opens up a hole and Big Dick rushes inside. Heavy bosom is still being pressed hard; Passionate Lady, Thighs, and Big Dick are still working hard. Bare Belly is under pressure.

In the stretch, Merry Widow cracks under the strain. Big Dick is making a hard drive. Bare Belly is close up, and it is Big Dick over Passionate Lady by a length.

At the finish, Big Dick is trying to shoot out in front, but Passionate Lady takes all he has and it looks like a dead heat. Heavy Bosom falls. Bare Belly is exhausted and Thighs pulls up. Clean Sheets never had a chance. Conscience never was a factor.

Flash!!! Big Dick made a squirt and wins by a head!!!

19

Mathematical Problem

If a pig drinks a quart of buttermilk before he starts, and runs a mile before he farts, and the farther he runs, the farther he gits; how far will he run before he shits?

The Solution

In order for you to win this bet, I must take you to where the fart was let.

A farmer said he saw the pig pass, with buttermilk shooting from his ass; the farmer was a mile from where the pig started, and the pig passed the farmer just after he farted.

'Twas so funny, the farmer just had to laugh, while the pig ran nearly a mile and a half.

Now if the pig is lucky and controls his gas, and can run for a mile with a puckered ass, it seems to me if he keeps his wits, he can run five miles before he shits.

Nature

Pussy is a nature,
It makes a man a fool,
It takes away his worries,
And wears away his tool,

When a man gets on a woman,
He hasn't long to stay,
His head is full of nonsense,
And his ass is full of play,

He gets on like a lion,
And gets off like a lamb,
And when he buttons up his pants,
He isn't worth a damn!

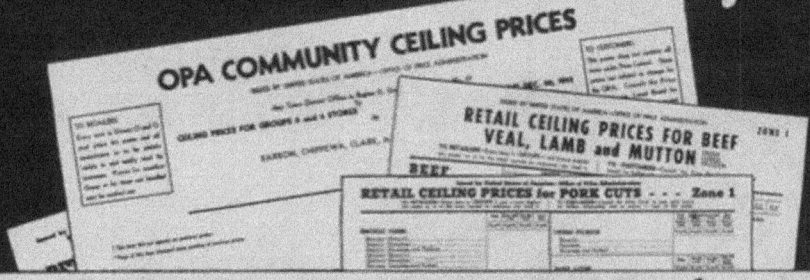

NEW CEILING PRICE LISTS ARE HERE!

Ask to see our copies

WE WILL EXPLAIN HOW YOU CAN USE THEM.....and how you can get copies of the lists for use at home.

CHECK SELLING PRICES WITH CEILING PRICES WHEN YOU SHOP

OFFICE OF PRICE ADMINISTRATION - UNITED STATES OF AMERICA

Prostitutes Union Local 69

UNITED ORDER OF CHEMISE LIFTERS, INC.

OUR MOTTO

"MAY WE HAVE OUR PIECE"

Fellow members:

Your organization has been informed that our market has recently been flooded with important "pussy" from the foreign countries who have been under pricing us. Therefore we have decided to reduce our rates.

Common hump	$1.00
(with pillow under ass, 50 cents extra)	
Back scuttle (dog fashion)	$1.50
Gobbling (french style)	$3.00
Up the dirt road	$.50
Diddling on edge of bed	$.75
Pullyer dummy	$.75
Saloon keepers & bartenders	$7.50
Police, firemen, & taxi drivers	$18.00
Chippies in prime condition	$5.00
Milk fed quiff	$10.00
with finger in asshole	$12.00
with french poodle licking balls	$15.00
Amateur whore with maidenhead	$25.00
Hallway rub	$.75
with door knob in asshole	$1.00
for extra wiggle add 10 cents to above prices	

A discount of fifty percent will be allowed for buttonhead peckers, otherwise known as twat robbers, liver disturbers, bowel movers, and long destroyers.

Those having more than 8 inch peckers should not patronize our members, as it is not in accordance with our by-laws.

Lotta Kunz, President
Ophelia Rass, Secretary
Eileen Back, Treasurer

The Night Shift Worker

Dear husband, dear husband, I tremble with fear,
You have been on the night shift for over a year,
And since you are gone nearly all of the night,
A good intercourse is far from my sight.

Husband dear, husband dear, don't be a fool,
Since working the night shift, you've ruined your tool,
You had better go hungry for the rest of your life,
Than to bring home a pecker, so soft, to your wife.

I was always so happy, as your little queen
But now at night you are never seen.
When you finally get home, so pale and so meek,
I just want to do things, but you go to sleep.

Each morning dear husband, when you go to bed,
Your intentions are good, but your pecker is dead.
I play with your pecker, so curled up and dry,
'Til I get so mad, I could lay down and cry.

I have pleaded dear husband, with tears in my eyes,
I have played with your balls, but your pecker won't rise.
I will get me a man who works through the day,
And at night while you are gone, I will really make hay.

In this whole wide world, there is only one sin,
For which there is no pardon, and never has been,
And that is when a man becomes so damned mean,
That he gives up his wife's screwing, to run a machine.

Urinal Typecasting

Fat man: uses the touch system because he cannot see over his belly, hits the bowl sometimes, but more often the floor or wall.

The braggart: opens three buttons when one would suffice.

Fastidious man: washes hands before. Uses dainty thumb and index finger grip. Washes hands after.

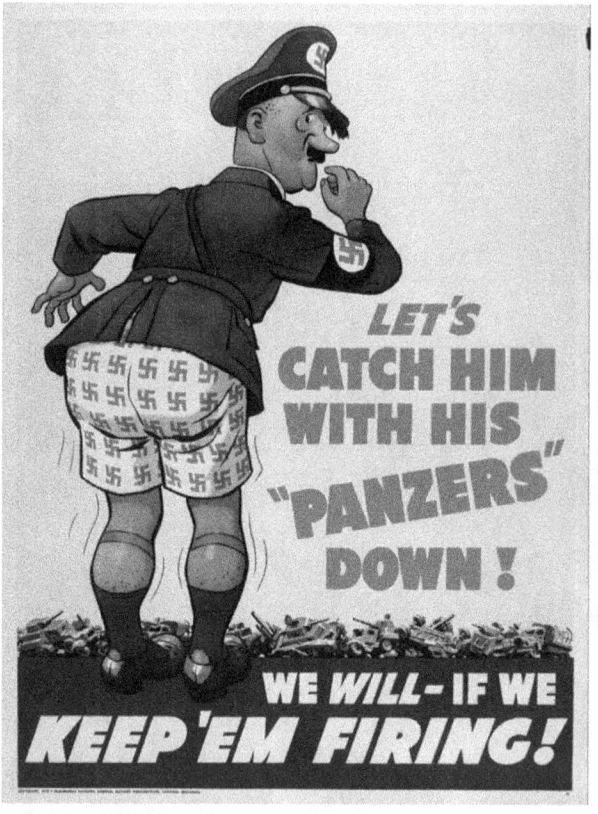

Canine man: gets the urge whenever he sees the "men." Dashes into washroom every fifteen minutes for a few drops. Likes to walk up and down urinals. A "gooser." Has dog blood in his veins. Loves trees and fire plugs.

Feminine man: sits down for the job.

Absentminded man: opens vest, takes out tie, sticks out tongue-pisses in his pants.

Excitable man: shorts have twisted around, cannot find hole. Rips pants in rage.

Sociable man: joins friends in urinating wheather he needs it or not.

Cross-eyed man: looks into urinal at left, leaks into one at right and flushes the one in the center.

Timid man: cannot urinate if anyone is watching. Flushes urinal pretending he has leaked, sneaks back later.

Indifferent man: all urinals being occupied, leaks into sink.

Nosey man: attempts to see into other urinal to see how other man is fixed.

Worried man: isn't sure that he has been in lately. Makes frenzied search and inspection.

Clever man: no hands. Shows off by adjusting necktie. Looks around for admiring glances.

Frivolous man: plays the stream up, down, and across the urinal. Attempts to hit fly. Never grows up.

Disgruntled man: stands in front of the urinal for awhile, then gives up. Walks out of washroom grumbling to himself.

Sneaky man: farts silently while leaking and acts innocent. Knows man in the next urinal will be blamed.

Personality man: tells dirty jokes while leaking and has pronounced control over farts. Has his friends in stiches.

Sloppy man: telltale wet drops always below fly. Never misses shoes. Usually walks out with fly open. Doesn't wash hands.

Childish man: leaks directly into pool at bottom of urinal. Likes to hear bubbling noise it makes.

Patient man: stands for incredible length of time waiting. Sometimes reads newspaper with free hand.

Efficient man: waits until he has to crap so he can do both at the same time.

Speedy man: rushes in and sprays countryside. Never fails to catch penis in zipper.

Methodical man: shakes carefully to last drop which always goes down pant leg.

Would be artist: tries to write name in snow but has to give up on last three letters in name.

A Shot In The Dark That Found Its Mark

A bunch of the boys were whooping it up,
In one of those Yukon halls,
The kid that handled the music box,
Was stealthily scratching his balls,

The faro kid had his hand on the box,
Of the lady known as Lou,
While down on the floor on top of a whore,
Lay dangerous Dan McGrew,

When out of the night that was black as a bitch,
And into the din and the smoke,
Stepped a shaky old prick just in from the crick,
With a rusty load in his poke,

As he shouldered his way through the mangy crowd,
He clutched the crotch of his pants,
He looked like a man with a dose of the clap,
In the last stage of St. Vitus' dance,

His trousers were split and covered with spit,
That looked like the white of an egg,
His balls hung low and swung to and fro,
Every time he moved his leg,

His face was as red as a baboon's ass,
As the passion within him burned,
Then he lugged out his cock to display to the flock,
And everyone's asshole squirmed,

In his ragged clothes, he stood ready to hose,
Any bitch who came his way,
He dangled his dong from his horny palm,
And howled that he wanted to play,

Then the lights went out and I ducked to the floor,
And the stranger sprang in the dark,
His aim was true and the sparks they flew,
As his donnicker found its mark,

Then with might and main and screams of pain,
A man's voice filled the room,
With sighs and moans and farts and groans,
Three forms were stacked in the gloom,

The lights came on and the stranger rose,
With a satisfied look on his pan,
And there on the floor with his asshole tore,
Lay poor old, cornholed Dan.

31

Know Your Scriptures

A Bronx commuter who had been riding the subway for several years and suffered many discomforts, finally became desperate and wrote the company; "Your service is so terrible, it is worse than traveling conditions 3,000 years ago."

The company replied, "You are evidently very unfamiliar with history, or you would know that 3,000 years ago the only means of traveling was on foot."

The commuter answered: "You are evidently ignorant of it, or you are a very poor Bible student. Chapter 16 says that Aaron rode to the city on his ass, and I'll be flamed if I've been able to do that in your cars in the last five years."

RELIGIOUS BOOK WEEK

MAY 6-13

READ BOOKS OF SPIRITUAL VALUE

NATIONAL CONFERENCE OF CHRISTIANS AND JEWS

House Hunting

A young couple who were about to be married were looking over a house in the country. After satisfying themselves that it was suitable they departed for home. During the return journey the young lady was very thoughtful, and when asked the reason for her silence she replied, "Did you notice the W.C. (water closet)?" He had not done so and upon returning home immediately wrote to the landlord inquiring where it was situated. The landlord didn't understand what W.C. meant and concluded that it meant the Wesleyan Church. He replied as follows:

Dear Sir,

I very much regret the delay in replying to your letter but have the pleasure of informing you that the W.C. is situated about nine miles from the house, and seats about 250 people. This is a very unfortunate thing if you are in the habit of going regularly, but no doubt you would be glad to know that a great many people make a day of it. Others who cannot spare the time go by auto and arrive just in time, but generally they are in such a hurry that they cannot wait. The last time my wife and I went was six years ago and we had to stand the whole time. It may interest you to know that a bazaar is to be given to furnish the W.C. with plush seats as the members feel that this is a long felt wait. I may mention that it pains me not to be able to go more often.

Sincerely yours,

Silas Jones

How to Kill an Eel

Little Johnny, ten years old, said to his mother, "Mom, what is a petting party?" His mother replied, "Well son, when I was young we called it courting. It is a long time since your pa and I courted, so if you hide behind the curtain some night when your sister Sally has her beau, you can find out." Johnny did this and the next day his mother said, "Well, Johnny, did you find out? You did? Well tell me."

"Well, Ma, Sally and Ed sat on the davenport and talked awhile, and then Ed held her hand and Sally leaned over and he kissed her several times.

After awhile Sally sat on his lap and Ed put both his arms around her and squeezed her awful hard and kissed her some more, but all the while he felt her boobies with one hand and put his other hand on her legs, at first; then on her knee, and then under her dress as far as I could see.

They both seemed to be getting excited about something and pretty soon Sally lay down on her back. Ed unbuttoned her dress and took out her boobies, played with them, and then began to kiss and suck them.

After several minutes of this he pulled her dress way up past her belly and, oh boy! You should see what she has between her legs. It must be wonderful the way Ed played with it. He felt all over it and Sally must have liked it because she spread her legs real wide and just laid there contented. But, ma, here's the real part. While Ed was feeling between her legs and kissing her belly, Sally reached down and unbuttoned his pants and out jumps a big eel about eight inches long and had a big head.

Sally got real excited because she thought it was getting away from her and held it real tight in her hands and tried to squeeze it to death, but she couldn't do it.

They were both working and panting and I heard Sally ask Ed to put it in her. So Ed got on top of Sally and put the eel in his hand and put the eel in a place that is covered with hair between Sally's legs.

He started to work up and down and shoved the eel all the way up in her belly and I guess Sally was afraid it would get away from her because she kept pushing her belly up to him every time he pulled it out a little. All the while Sally was panting and moaning and they were both working as hard as they could to kill the eel.

After a couple of minutes Sally got real wild and excited and they both lay still for awhile and Ed got off her. They sure killed the eel, ma, because I could see there was no life in the eel anymore. The eel's head hung low and Sally looked at it as though she had killed it and told Ed that she loved it.

So you see, Ma, it's a funny thing. First she kills it and then she tells Ed she loves it. Isn't it funny though, Ma?"

And about this time Johnny saw his mother put her hand in her lap, press real hard, and look real funny.

A Dissertation On Men

Men are what women marry. They have two feet, two hands and sometimes two wives, but they never have more than one dollar or one idea at a time. Like Turkish cigarettes, men are all made of the same material; the only difference is that some are better disguised than others.

Generally speaking, men may be divided into two classes, husbands and bachelors. An eligible bachelor is a man of obstinancy entirely surrounded by suspicion. Husbands are of three varieties: prizes, surprises, and consolation prizes!

Making a husband out of a man is one of the highest plastic arts known to civilization. It requires science, sculpture, common sense, the ability to see and not see, hope, faith and charity, a good bed and a strong backbone. Besides, husbands bear a startling resemblance to a certain well known four footed animal that has to be kept on a strong leash or it will run after every cat that comes along.

It is a psychological marvel that a soft, fluffy, tender, violet scented, sweet thing, like a woman, should enjoy kissing a big, awkward, stubby chinned, tobacco and bay-rum scented, thing, like a man, but women do it every time and come back for more. If you believe man in everything you cease to interest him and if you argue with him in everything, you cease to charm him. If you believe all he tells you, he thinks you are a fool, and if you don't he thinks you are a cynic. If you flatter a man, it frightens him

to death; if you don't you bore him to death. If you permit him to make love to you, he gets tired of you in the end. But if you don't, he gets tired of you in the beginning. If you wear gay color rouge and a startling hat, he hesitates to take you out, but if you sport a little brown toque and a tailored suit, he takes you out and stares at every woman in gay colors, rouge and a startling hat, all evening. A man loves to stare at a woman's legs when her back is turned so you can tell that he is interested if he turns around for a look at a woman whom he has been speaking to on the street. If you join him in the gayeties of life and approve of his smoking ad drinking, he swears you are driving him to the devil, but if you don't, he vows that you are snobbish and too nice. If you are the clinging vine type he doubts whether you have any brains, and if you are a modern, advanced, independent woman, he doubts whether you have a heart. In short, a man is just another worm of the dust. He comes along, wiggles about for awhile, and finally some chicken gets him!

Basic Definitions 101

Adolescence: An intermediate stage between puberty and adultery.

Adultery: Two wrong people doing the right thing.

Alimony: The screwing you get for the screwing you got.

Baby Carriage: Last year's fun on wheels.

Bastard Fart: A little stinker without a pop.

Brassiere: A device that makes molehills out of mountains.

Castrated Dinosaur: A colossal fossil with a docile tassel.

Complicated: A confused situation that makes it hard to get at the work, like a knock-kneed virgin.

Conscience: That which hurts when everything else feels good.

Cream Puff: A pregnant cookie.

Divorce: Something that happens when two people can't stomach each other.

Enema: A goose with a flush.

Engagement Ring: A learner's permit.

Eskimo: A frigid midget with a rigid digit.

Horse Show: A lot of horses showing their asses to a lot of horses-asses showing their horses.

Kiss: Uptown shopping for downtown business.

Kiss 2: Sabotage before invasion.

Maternity Dress: A draped crepe over a raped shape.

Maternity Dress 2: A "zoot suit" with a "rape shape."

Metallurgist: A man who can take one look at a platinum blonde and tell whether she is "virgin steel" or "common ore."

Mistress: Something between a mattress and a mister.

Morning: The time of day when the rising generation retires; and the retiring generation rises.

Mother's Day: Nine months after "father's night."

Nurse: A pan handler.

Nursery: A place to park last year's fun until it grows a bit.

Old Maid: A girl who has advanced in years, who has gone through life with no runs, no hits and no errors, presumably.

Outdoor Girl: One with the bloom of youth on her cheeks and the cheeks of youth in her bloomers.

Papoose: Consolation prize for taking a chance on an Indian blanket.

Passion: A feeling you feel when you feel you are going to feel a feeling you never felt before.

Petticoat: A drop curtain for the greatest amusement place in the world.

Pregnancy: A woman swelled up over her mate's handiwork.

Prostitute: A busy body.

Pajamas: Items of clothing that newlyweds place by their beds in case of fire.

Pansy: One who likes his vice-versa.

Pimp: Out of necessity, a "crack salesman."

Private Secretary: A good private secretary is one who never misses a period.

Psychiatrist: A man who tries to find out if infants have more fun in infancy than adults have in adultery.

Rape: Seduction without salesmanship.

Sob Sister: A girl who sits on your lap and bawls, making it hard for you.

Spring Fever: When the iron in your blood turns to lead in your pants.

Triplets: Taking seriously what was poked at you in fun.

Virgin Sheep: One that can run faster than the shepherd.

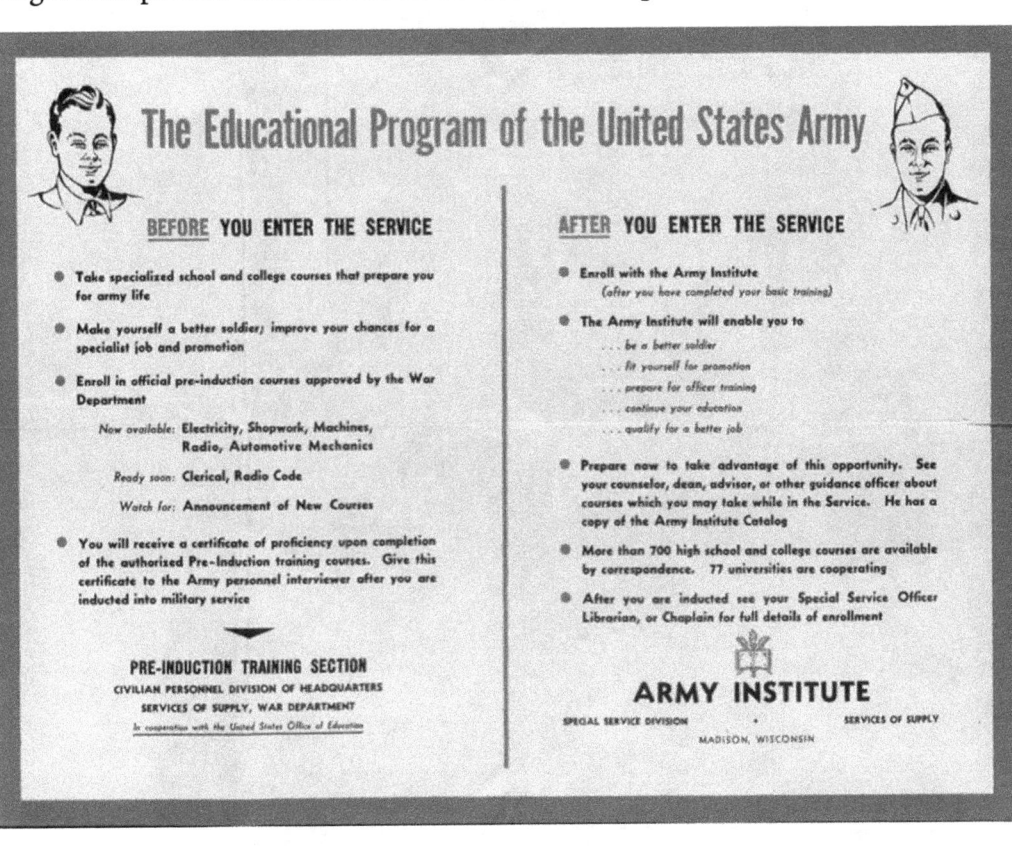

40

Oriental Wisdom

Men with little hole in pocket feel cocky; men with big hole in pocket feel nuts.

He who lays girl on hill is not on the level.

Scotchman who keeps money in jockstrap has it guarded by private dick.

Man who kisses womens breast gets bust in mouth.

He who takes seven day honeymoon makes one hole week.

Women with small hips-uncanny.

He who wants to raise chickens must have cock and pullet.

Woman who cooks carrots and peas in same pot very unsanitary.

He who lays wife on floor gets permanent fixture.

Tacks on floor not so good, screw in bed, damn good.

He who keeps money in jockstrap gets finances all balled up.

He who has acrobatic finger makes broad jump.

Young man climb tree to get cherries, wise man spread limbs.

Zipperphobia

A curse upon those who mix science with clothes,
Improvements on pants are the cause of my woes,
For my sweetheart has left me since Saturday night,
Sartorial splendor gave birth to my plight.

It was dark in the hallway, the lady was willing,
We were ready for action, not cooing or billing,
When right at the crux, where I should be most chipper,
Goddamn it, my pecker got caught in my zipper.

Oh woe to each genius of cog wheels and cams,
And woe to the men who apply all such shams,
Mechanical skill is all right for the wise,
But it's painful as hell when adapted to flies.

My sweetheart has left me and hopes that I roast,
She said that I failed when she needed me most,
God knows that I never intended to gyp her,
Goddamn it, my pecker got caught in my zipper.

So woe to all tailors who meddle with science,
And woe to all gadgets that woo our reliance,
Machines are all right for the technical guys,
But they're painful as hell when they're sewed into flies.

The zipper's all right but not for the male,
Whose one aim in life is getting his tail,
In women's ensemble it fills a real need,
So take them off pants for comfort and speed!

Women . . . our wounded need your care!

YOU can serve as medical technicians, surgical technicians, and in other Army hospital assignments

Join a hospital company

OTHER ASSIGNMENTS AVAILABLE AT ARMY AIR FORCES, GROUND FORCES, AND SERVICE FORCES INSTALLATIONS

WOMEN'S ARMY CORPS

For information apply to any U. S. Army Recruiting Station or your local Postmaster

"*I fear all we have done is awaken a sleeping giant and fill him with a terrible resolve.*" ~*Admiral Isoroku Yamamoto*

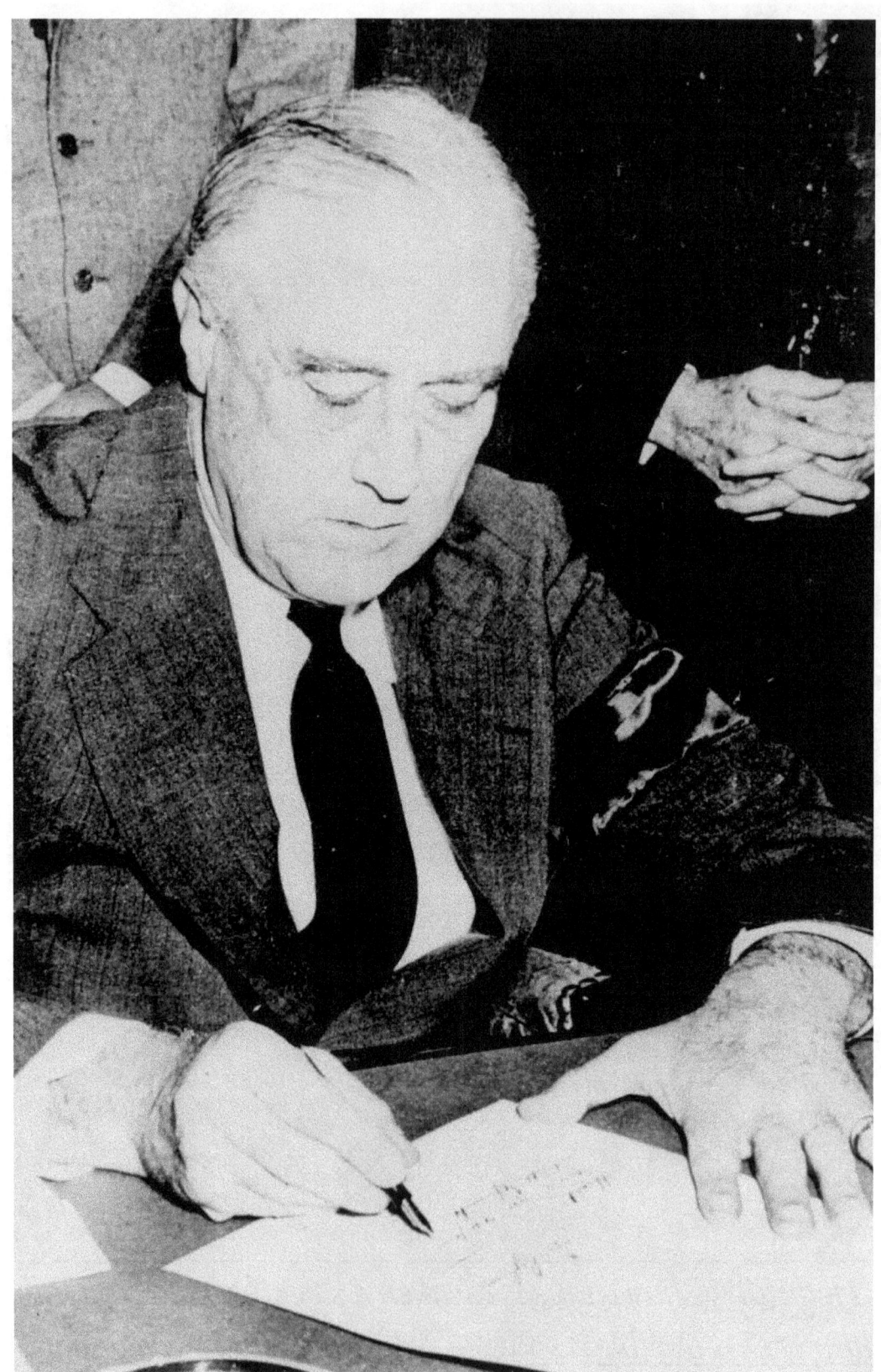

FDR signs Declaration of War against Japan on December 8, 1941 (opposite page). Propaganda poster by Ben Shahn (above). Eisenhower gives the order of the Day to paratroopers in England on June 6, 1944 (below).

Women were essential to the war effort. Poster by J. Howard Miller (above.)

Real life Rosie the Riveters: Lockheed riveter (inset, above) and workers at Marinship Corp.

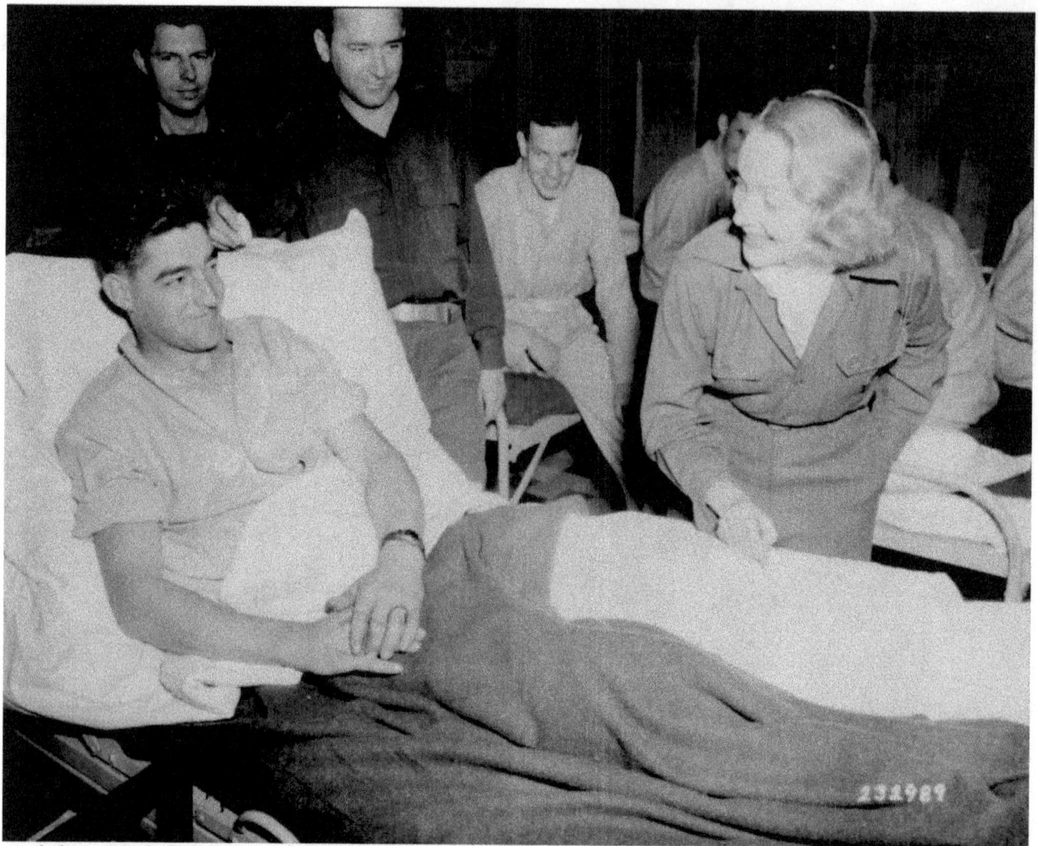

Celebrities did their part too: Rita Hayworth (opposite); Marlene Dietrich (above); Bing Crosby (below).

PLEASE DRIVE CAREFULL
MY BUMPERS ARE ON THE SCRAP H

Nose art pinups. USAAF photos.

Pearl Harbor Attack: USS Arizona (top, Official U.S. Navy Photo, now in National Archives); USS Shaw (bottom, U.S. Naval History and Heritage Command Photograph).

Keitel signs surrender in Berlin (above). and Victory celebration in Picadilly, May 7, 1945 (opposite). Below, luxury ocean liner Queen Mary returns troops to New York, June 20, 1945.

Raising of flag at Iwo Jima, February 23, 1945 (above). USS Missouri and fighters fly in formation during surrender ceremonies (below).

President Truman announces Japan's surrender at White House, August 14, 1945 (above). MacArthur signs documents at surrender ceremonies Sept. 2, 1945 (below).

"All right, they're on our left, they're on our right, they're in front of us, they're behind us . . . they can't get away this time."

~Lt. General Lewis B. "Chesty " Puller

"An Army is a team; lives, sleeps, eats, fights as a team. This individual heroic stuff is a lot of crap."

~General George S. Patton, Jr.

Tee For Two

A young couple just got married and on their honeymoon John told Marsha that she would not be his first girl; and he told her that if she wanted to confess any previous behavior he should know about that he would forgive her in order to start an honest marriage.

Marsha confessed her love of her high school sweetheart and said that otherwise she had not been promiscuous, with only one exception.

When a National golf tournament had come to her town she confessed she had a one night stand with one of the famous golfers. This however was a one time thing only, she assured John.

John was satisfied with this, as he said he would not have turned down a famous movie star if he had the chance.

And so they went one time around the bed and John reached over to pick up the phone by the bed stand. Marsha reached over immediately and put her hand on his arm and said "Honey what are you doing? to which he replied, I'm calling the front desk for a bottle of champagne! She then replied, "But the golfer didn't do that. He then said, "What exactly did he do then? She stated, "He rolled me over and did it again!"

Well, not to be outdone, John began again to make love to Marsha. After it went on for quite some time they finally came together half exhausted, and again John reached over for the phone. Marsha again held on to his arm and said "Excuse me, but if you are calling for the champagne that's not what the golfer did! "Well exactly what did he do now? "Well he just rolled me over and did it again!

And so John had no other choice but to try to satisfy her again. The bed heaved to and fro, up and down, and sometimes even sideways. Finally in one big gasp and an "Oh My" scream, the bed broke under them as they finally came.

Completely exhausted Marsha wearily said, "Are you going to call down for the champagne?" To which John replied, "Hell NO! I'm calling that golfer. I want to know what par this hole is!"

The Wrong Package

Jenny *on the job*

Wears styles designed for Victory

A young man went into a department store to buy a pair of gloves for his sweetheart. At the same counter a young lady was buying a suit of underwear for herself. By some mistake the parcels got mixed and the young man got the underwear and sent it to his sweetheart, instead of the gloves with the following letter:

Dear Marie,

I am enclosing you a little gift which I hope you will accept in the place of the ones I ripped last night. I hope no other hands than mine will ever touch them. I should like to be with you when you try them on, and help you button them up.

Always blow in them before putting them on. If they are too large you can let them wrinkle down, as a great many girls wear them that way.

Be careful that some fellow with dirty hands doesn't soil them, but yet you can clean them with benzine. The saleslady told me she had worn a pair just like them for two years and never had them cleaned.

Do not take them off on the street or while in the streetcar as your skin chaps very easily.

With love,
Jack

Foods that count keep him on the job

Recipe for Banana Nut Cake

Take an armful of well formed girl, two laughing blue eyes and cherry lips, squeeze until quite warm. Then add a little moonlight to suit the taste; add a little spooning to make it rise. When good and hot put in the banana. Work up and down gently until the banana begins to cream, then quickly add the nuts. The results will be astonishing; two rolled up eyes, a sigh of relief and the cake is finished. Sit out on the porch to cool.

Over the Hill

It's not the gray hair that makes a man old,
Or the far-away stare in his eye, so I'm told.
But when the mind makes a contract the body can't fill,
You're over the hill, brother, you're over the hill.

When you look on a Venus and just heave a sigh,
When you hear a bum joke and laugh 'til you cry,
When it's all in the head, and you've lost the old thrill,
You're over the hill, brother, you're over the hill.

You can fool the dear wife with the cleverest lies,
Shear the dear lamb and pull wool over her eyes;
But when she calls for an encore and you claim you're ill,
You're over the hill, brother, you're over the hill.

This life is a conflict, the battle is keen,
There's just so many shots in the old magazine,
When you've used the last shot and you can't refill,
You're over the hill, brother, you're over the hill.

Salvage the engine, old boy, if you can,
For Lydia Pinkham's can't help out a mere man,
You can't get a gland from a little pink pill,
You're over the hill, brother, you're over the hill.

This is my story alas and alack,
When you've squeeze out the creme, you can't put it back,
If you want to make whoopee, then don't wait until,
You're over the hill, brother, you're over the hill.

Suzanne

Suzanne was a girl with plenty of class,
who knocked them all dead when she wiggled her

eyes at the fellows as girls sometimes do,
to make it quite plain that she wanted to

go to a movie or go for a sail,
and then hurry home for a nice piece of

cake or pie or a slice of roast duck,
for after each meal she was ready to

go for a walk or a stroll on the dock,
with any young man with a sizeable

roll of bills or plenty of front,
and if he was willing she'd show him her

little white dog, who was subject to fits,
and then she might let him take hold of her

little white hands with a movement so quick,
she'd reach right over and tickle his

chin, as she asked for a trick learned in France,
and then she would ask him to take off his

coat, while she sang of the Mandalay shore,
for whatever she was, Suzanne was no bore.

A Short, Short Story

The Hotel Astor hired a new bus driver and instructed him to meet all incoming trains and announce at the depot in a loud voice "Free bus to Hotel Astor." On the way to the station on his first trip, he kept repeating to himself "Free bus to Hotel Astor" until he had it memorized perfectly.

Upon arrival at the station he became confused at all of the noise and started shouting, "Free hotel at bust your astor! I mean, free ass at the hotel buster! I mean, freeze your ass at the hotel buster! I mean bust your ass at hotel freezer! Oh slit, take the trolley car!"

The Midnight Ride of Paul Revere

Listen my children and you shall hear,
Of the midnight ride of Paul Revere.
Paul was a sturdy man and strong,
With a pecker that hung like a mighty prong.

Why the damned thing hung clear to his sock,
Like a pendulum on an eight-day clock;
It was wrinkled and notched, but stood the gaff,
and damn near split a dame in half.

Came a night, when Paul, in his cups of gin,
Found the mighty prong beneath his chin.
"What the hell", he said as he forced it down,
"This means a midnight ride to town."

So he cranked his ford while the pale moon grinned,
Leaped to the wheel and away he spinned.

He hit the hills and dales in high,
With his mind set on a dead pig's eye.
'Till with grinding brakes he hit the town,
Where he raced hell bent for Amelia Brown.

Now Amelia, cradled all of the local cock,
In a crotch shaped on a butchers block.
But she knew damn well when she lamped at Paul,
that as big as it was, she needed it all.

With a pig-like squeal and a thankful moan,
Revere peeled down and shoved Steve home.

GIVE HIM A WHIFF OF HIS OWN B.O.*

*BLITZKRIEG OFFENSIVE

KEEP 'EM FIRING!

While Amelia grunted like a bashful bride,
And prayed he'd leave his nuts outside.

The bout proceeded till early morn,
When Amelia vowed her twat was torn;
So Paul climbed off a bit uncertain,
And swabbed Steve down on the parlor curtain.

As he reeled Steve into his BVD's,
The room reeked strong with the smell of cheese;
He tucked four bits into the bureau drawer,
Let a ripping fart and slammed the door.

While Amelia struggled to get out of bed,
Got one good whiff and ducked her head,
Underneath the sheets with an awful groan,
While Revere rolled down the road to home.

House Cleaning

I had twelve bottles of whiskey in my cellar and my wife told me to empty the contents of each bottle down the sink, "or else." So I said I would and proceeded with the unpleasant task.

I withdrew the cork from the first bottle and poured the contents down the sink, with the exception of one glass which I drank. I extracted the cork from the second bottle and poured the contents down the sink with the exception of one glass which I drank. I then withdrew the cork from the third bottle and emptied the good ole booze down the sink, except a glass which I drank. I pulled the cork from the fourth sink and poured the bottle down the glass which I drank.

I pulled the bottle from the cork of the next and drank one sink out of it and poured the rest down the glass. I pulled the next cork out of it and poured the rest down the glass. I pulled the next cork out of my throat and poured the sink down the bottle and drank the glass. Then I corked the sink with the glass, bottled the drink and drank the pour.

When I had everything emptied I steadied the house with one hand, counted the bottles and corks and glasses with the other, Which were 29. To be sure I counted them again and I had 74. As the house came by, I counted them again, and when they came by finally I had the houses and bottles and corks and glasses counted except one house and one bottle, which I drank.

Say fellow, I've got the wifiest little nice you ever saw.

The China Problem

Chinese "hoolay, hoolay!"

Chinese couple very wild,
Want to have a pure white child,
Seek advice, what can be done?
But find no way of having one.

Watch TV and while they sit,
Find a way of doing it,
On the job without delay,
Sideways in the Chinese way.

Baby born, oh great delight,
Little devil is all white,
Father proud and full of glee,
Talk what he saw on TV.

Hoolay, hoolay, me no foolee,
Me put Tide on my toolee.
Wifee also very fussy,
She put Rinso on her pussy.

"You wonder where the yellow went?
Me brushee balls with pepsodent!!!"

Three chinese sisters who aren't married:

Tu-yung-tu, Tu-dumb-tu, and No-yen-tu

Three chinese sisters who can't get a date:

Ug-li, Home-li, and Sic-li

Did You Hear About?

The moron who was feeling so low, he got his face slapped.

The moron who cut off his left side so that he would be all right.

The moron who cut a hole in the rug because he wanted to see the floor show.

The moron that sat in the middle of the street with two pieces of bread in his hands waiting for a traffic jam, when along came a streetcar and gave him a jar.

The moron who thought Peter Pan was a toilet.

The moron that married a colored woman so his children could have chocolate milk.

The moron that was necking with his girlfriend under a toadstool because he thought it was a mushroom.

The moron who pushed a cow off a cliff because he wanted to see the jersey bounce.

The two bald-headed morons that put their head together, and made an ass out of themselves.

The dying moron who put a chair by the side of his bed for rigor mortis to set in.

The moron that cut the toilet seat in half when he heard that his halfassed relatives were coming to see him.

The moron that took the clock to bed with him because he heard it was fast.

The moron that starts a story, "Once upon a girl I had a time."

The moron that took a ruler to bed with him to see how long he slept.

The moron that took a bale of hay to bed with him to feed his nightmare.

The moron that took his pregnant wife to the grocery store because he heard they had a free delivery.

The moron that put bread crumbs in his shoes to feed his pigeon toes.

The moron who jumped off the Empire State Building to show everyone he had guts.

The moron who was afraid to die, so he went into the living room.

The moron who got off the street-car backwards because he heard a lady say she was going to grab his seat when he got off.

The moron who watered his victory garden with whiskey so he could have stewed tomatoes.

The moron who cut off his arms so he could wear a sleeveless sweater.

The moron who went outside in the morning and said, "Gee it feels nice out, guess i'll leave it out."

What the two morons did on their wedding night? Nothing!

The moron that was lying in a ditch, who propped his head up on the curb to get his mind out of the gutter.

The moron that was a sculptor; he put his model to bed and chiseled on his wife.

Get the Good...
FROM FRUIT

• Use fruit juice *fresh*.... if it has to stand, keep covered and cold.

• Cook in the peel if you can....if you must peel, make it thin.

2   BUREAU of HOME ECONOMICS
U.S. DEPARTMENT of AGRICULTURE

A Thief in the Night

Here's to the moments that are stolen,
And stealing is certainly wrong.
But after those moments are taken,
To whom do they really belong?

For if my wife ne'er comes to claim them,
And your husband ne'er makes a fuss,
Let's hold our heads up proudly,
And say they belong to us.

For if you had bushels of apples,
And left them alone to rot,
And a neighbor came along and ate them,
Would you blame him? Certainly not.

For apples were made to be eaten,
And moments were made for delight.
And that's what we'll tell our conscience,
If it keeps us awake at night.

A German Christmas

Der night vas Krismus und it vas still,
Der stockings vas hung, expectink der fill,
Undt nodding vas stirring, nodt efen a louse,
For fear dot St. Nick voulf nix cumerouse.
Mudder said, "Children, go by der bedt,"
Then tucked them tight in and kissed their head.
She lifts der night dress to carry der toys,
Who vas peeking, it vas der liddle boys,
Mama's night gown was up in der face,
Undt der children could see a big bare space,
Hans said, "Mudder, we see der toys in der lap,
But for who is der liddle fur cap?"
Mama said, "Shush!", undt she laff oudt right,
"I think I giff dot to your papa tonite."

Le Foque Restaurant

Proprietors: I.P. Freely & G. Howie Phartz

Menu

Soup
Cream of Maiden Pea ~ Fartless Muffled Bean

Entrees
Seasoned Twats on Toast ~ Titty-pink Nipples

Roasts
Broiled Tits with French Dressing
Brochettes of Testicles, Muff Diver's
Boneless Peckers, Elderly
Enlarged Ovaries with Asshole Brown Gravy

Vegetables
Reamed Spinach ~ Buttered Snatch

Salad
Chef's Surprise
He tried to goose our pretty waitress!

Desserts
Ass Cheeks a la Crème ~ After Dinner Mints, Blue Balls
Frozen Jocks ~ Chilled Menstruation

Liquors
Champagne ~ Frizzyass
Enlarged Dubin Prix ~ Cognac

Coffee ~ Demitasse

Music by our famous Kotex Serenaders playing ragtime. Listen to the famous
theme song, "When it's Kotex time in Pussyville, Little Dickie won't be there!"
Souvenirs and favors by our pretty hostess, miss Ophelia Pratt, who furnishes
rubbers to the gents on request.
Our chef won the Grande Prix in Italy!
Visit the Russian room and see Ivan Tearhertitsoff.

The Wolf

If he parks his little flivver,
Down beside the moonlit river,
And you feel him start to quiver,

He's a wolf.

If he says your gorgeous looking,
That your dark eyes set him cooking,
But your eyes aren't where he's looking,

He's a wolf.

When he says that you're an eyeful,
But his hands begin to trifle,
And his heart pumps like a rifle,

He's a wolf.

If by chance you start a-kissin,
And you feel his heart a-missin,
And you plead but he won't listen,

He's a wolf.

If his arms are strong like sinews,
And he stirs the gypsy in you,
So that you want him agin' you,

Baby - you're the wolf!

83

The She Wolf

If she throws her little quiver,
In the front seat of your fliver,
And says, it's pleasant on the river

Brother, she's a wolf.

If the get up that she's a wearing,
Turns your head and keeps you staring,
Cause the length's a little daring,

Brother, she's a wolf.

If she really is bewitching,
If she kisses with a twitching,
As if her rose red lips were itching,

Brother, she's a wolf.

If she really lets you pet her,
Lets you snuggle in her sweater,
And you really think your better,

Brother, be a wolf!

A Soldier's Dream

A little maiden passing by,
A little winking of the eye
A little smile, a little date,
To meet you when the hour is late,

A little promise not to tell,
A little room in some hotel,
A little fussing on some chair,
A little tousling of the hair,

A little drink, a hand caress,
A little question, answer "yes",
A little shirtwaist laid aside,
A little breast that tried to hide,

A little hand that went a stealing,
A little pleased with a funny feeling,
A little coaxing and a little teasing,
An arm revealing that is most appealing,

A pair of panties mostly lace,
A little blush upon the face,
A little shading of the light,
A little bed with sheets so white,

A little loving in the gloom,
A little sigh, a quiet room.
A pair of lips so warm and wet,
A little whisper, "please, not yet."

A little pillow from the head,
Slipped beneath the hips instead,
A little effort to begin,
A little help to get it in,

Two little arms that grip me tight,
And then I whisper, "Does it feel all
right?",
She smiles and says, "It feels so good",
And then I reply "I thought it would."

Two little legs around me twine,
Two happy eyes look into mine,
A little movement to and fro,
A little "ah" a little "oh",

A little surge of something hot,
A little whisper, "all you've got?",
Two little hearts beat as one,
Two little lovers having fun,

A little effort to repeat,
A little spot upon the sheet,
A little shower when we are through,
A little drink, maybe two,

A little sleep and finally then,
A breakfast in bed at half past ten,
A little bill, a little tip,
A porter wishing a pleasant trip,

A little weariness the next day,
Like little children after play,
A little wish that you and I,
May have another by and by.

SOLDIERS *without guns*

Panning the Bedpan

When I had my operation I displayed a lot of guts,
I could take it, smile and like it, but the bedpan drove me nuts.
When nature called I'd call the nurse, and when I called she ran,
And soon I'd have my carcass parked upon that goddamn pan.

I'd slide back on my shoulders, but the leverage wasn't there,
And instead of doing something, I'd shoot a flock of air.
And when at last I'd get results, I'd feel around my seat,
To see if I had missed the pan and piled it on the sheet.

There was cold sweat on my forehead when I'd feel with cautious care,
And with sighs of satisfaction discover nothing there.
But now a new contortion would leave me weak and pale,
I'd have to bridge and twist and squirm to wipe my poor sore tail.

The muscles of my neck would bulge as I stood upon my head,
I'd make a few wild passes and fall weakly back in bed.
And when I'd ring, the nurse hopped in and carried off the pan,
And I'd wonder why, on such a job, they didn't send a man.

Then finally I'd settle down; that movement was a treat,
But wait a minute, what's so warm and wet upon the sheet?
With a look of apprehension I'd slowly raise my gown,
And there beneath my setter would be a blotch of brown.

And so, as operations go, I haven't any dread,
but gosh, it really burns me up to defecate in bed!

Observations

Modesty has ruined more kidneys than alcohol.

There will be slight changes in infant wear from day to day.

She was a test-pilot's girl friend. That's why I met her in a dive.

New health rule: wash face in morning and neck at night.

Who wouldn't like to be a hula dancer in Hawaii? All they do is sit around and twiddle their tums!?

Visitor: "How do you tell the ganders from the geese?"

Farmer: "Oh, we never worry about that. We just turn 'em loose and let 'em figure things out for themselves."

I want to get a brassiere for my wife.
Yes sir. What bust?
Nothing. It just wore out.

"One moment, lady," said the lisping clerk, "I'll hafta look up your thighs."

Entires in a diary:

Dec. 26. Snowin'. Can't go huntin.
Dec. 27. Still snowin'. Can't go huntin.
Dec. 28. Still snowin'. Shot grandmaw.

A lady asked her doctor - "Do you think raw oysters are healthy?" The doctor replied, "Yes, I never knew one to complain."

A dogs's philosophy of life:

If you can't eat it and you can't mount it, piss on it!

Then there was the country girl that was sent home from the country fair because she couldn't keep her calves together.

HE'S WATCHING YOU

Political Speech of a Prominent Lady

"We must have what men have. It may not be long, but we must have it!

If we cannot get it without friction, then we will have it with friction, or combinations, or both if necessary.

We refuse to be poked in the gallery any longer and insist on being placed on the floor of the House.

We are willing to look up to the man but we don't always want to be forced or held or held down without making a few motions of our own.

We want to hold up our end and show man possibilities whenever anything arises that will meet our expectations. Nothing that comes will be too hard for us.

We women have always been interested in good movements, and will take any load given us.

We are still willing to work under men that have been over us in the past, even to the point of exhaustion if necessary, but we are beginning to become disgusted with failings and shortcomings.

Never when anything arose that required our presence and attention have we failed to come again and again if the occasion required it,

But all too often our hopes have been met with feeble performances which have left us disappointed and unsatisfied.

How often have our efforts to push forward our ends been met in the House with the cry, "Up with the petticoats!"?

Now I say, "Up with the petticoats and down with the pants!"

As long as women are split the way they are, the men will always be on top!

Thank you, my friends."

Excerpts

From letters that have arrived at U.S. Government Bureaus from women asking allotments or correcting their applications:

"My husband has worked on his shift for about a month, and now he left me and I ain't had no pay since he has gone or before either."

"Both sides of my parents is poor and I can't expect nothing from them as my mother has been in bed with the same doctor for one year and won't change."

"Please send me a letter and tell me if my husband made application for a wife and baby."

"I have already had no clothing for this year and have been regularly visited by the clergy."

"You changed my little boy to a girl. Does this make any difference?"

"I am told that my husband sets in the YMCA every night with the piano playing in his uniform. I think you will find him there."

"Please send me my husband's form to fill out."

"I have already wrote to the President and if I don't hear from you, I will write to Uncle Sam and tell him about you both."

"This is my eighth child. What are you going to do about it?"

"In accordance with your instructions, I have given birth to twins in the enclosed envelope. I am forwarding the marriage certificate and birth certificate. One is a mistake."

"it ALL
depends on
ME"

PLEASE DON'T ASK TO HAVE IT WRAPPED

DECLARE A

PAPER HOLIDAY

FOR THE DURATION

SAVE {
WRAPPING PAPER

PAPER BAGS

WASTE PAPER

PAPER HAS GONE TO WAR

WAR PRODUCTION BOARD

No. 655 - Toilet Paper Rationing Form

Application for bowel movement.

1. Name in full_____
2. Age _____ address _____
3. Sex Male ( ) Female ( ) Other ( )
4. Where born _____
5. Is your house modern? Yes ( ) No ( )
6. What conveniences have you? Thunder Jug ( ) Indoor Toilet ( )
7. If Thunder Jug, one or two handles? 1( ) 2( )
8. What do you use? Toilet paper( ) Corncob ( )
              Newspaper ( ) Catalogue( )
9. Are you a Dribbler ( ) Chunker ( ) Strainer( )
   Whistler ( ) Meditator ( ) Grunter ( )
10. Is it Hard( ) Soft ( ) Runny ( ) Sloppy ( )
11. Color._____
12. Do you crap at home? Yes ( ) No ( )
13. Do you have obstructions that would hinder or impede a free and easy passage of a good turd? Such as piles? _____
14. Are you troubled with dysentery? Yes() No()
15. Do you have to use: Epsom Salts() Castor Oil()
    Lydia Pinkhams() Sulphur-Molasses()
16. During the fiscal year just past, how many times did your bowels move each quarter? _____
    Loose? ( ) Congealed? ( )
17. On December 31, 1943, how many bowel movements took place from the first of the year?_____
18. Approximately how many rolls of toilet paper were used up to December 31, 1943?_____
19. You will be allowed 65% of your last years bowel movement. If you for any reason will be unable to comply with the rules set forth in your ration book, you may appeal to you're nearest ration board. They will be sitting on the throne. We must conserve toilet paper! Our local boards have stopped straining themselves because there are too many assholes to go around, even in Washington. Save! Save! On toilet paper and win the war!
20. If for any reason you are robbed or lose your ration book or coupon, notify the authorities ar once. Guards will be placed at all outhouses to prevent unlawful crapping and waste of paper.

Slogan: a crap in time is fine — but crap on ration time!!

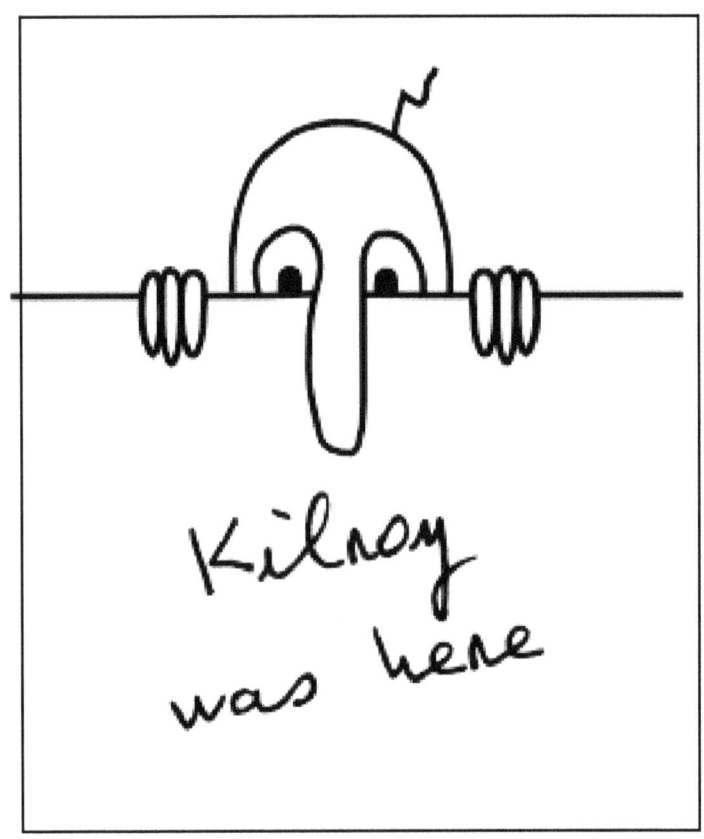

Plate Index

Interested in Publishing?

Do you have stories, pictures, photos of memorabilia or other items from this era? We'd love to hear from you. If you need help publishing, editing, or printing your material, drop us a line explaining what services you need. Please do not submit a manuscript. We do not accept blind submissions.

Email us at contact@postmortempublications.com or write to us at: P. O. Box 1007, Groveland, FL 34736.

Visit Our Website

Are you a collector or seller of WWII memorabilia? Be sure to visit our website's classified ad section.

www.postmortempublications.com

www.ingramcontent.com/pod-product-compliance
Lightning Source LLC
Chambersburg PA
CBHW071917160426
42813CB00098B/724